Breezes and Storms

Verse and Prose

Taysir N. Nashif

Printed in the United States of America.

ISBN: 978-1-4669-5300-0 (sc)
ISBN: 978-1-4669-5299-7 (e)

Trafford rev. 08/14/2012

 www.trafford.com

North America & international
toll-free: 1 888 232 4444 (USA & Canada)
phone: 250 383 6864 ♦ fax: 812 355 4082

Contents

Preface.. vii

Oh, Human Dignity 1

The Vine Tree Is My Home 2

New Orleans Is My Home.. 3

I Have a Skill... 5

Can We Rejoice.. 6

On You, O, Children of Africa, My Tears I Shed 7

Tears Are Falling on Humanity... 10

My Homeland.. 11

With My Pen I have Fenced-In My Garden.......................... 12

My Brother, Don't Deny Me the Warmth of Humanity.......... 13

Come 15

Deep Sadness 16

Our Feet Are Bleeding.. 17

A Raven of Separation 18

The Clusters of My Grape Garden Are Generous................... 19

Marching to the Hill of Virtue 20

Let Us Be Free... 21

Freedom 23

A Song for Peace in the Holy Land...................................... 24

To Humanity 26

To the Forest 27

Waves Have Not Drowned My Small Boat............................ 28

Trees of Evergreen Cypress 29

Your Big Sea of Love.. 30

Calm of the Sea... 31

Melting the Ice 32

Peace of Mind 33

Tranquility of Nature 34

My Writing Pen Cannot Draw My Image 35

A Kiss in the Dark.. 36

Days Have Gone By.. 37

Wails of Humanity... 38

Emptiness... 39
My Sense of Humanity Is Stronger 40
The Great Sea 41
The Great Shore of Jaffa 42
To the Sea of Jaffa... 43
Traversing the Desert... 44
At Sunset.. 45
I Stood, Looking Out.. 46
O, Myself.. 47
My Being 48
Uncertainty of the Self 49
The Mother 50
Love of Nature 52
My Young Woman Is Dancing for the Moon......................... 53
My Beloved 54
The Home and the Olive Tree 55
Autumn of the Hearts 56
O Moon.. 57
Loss of the Oases 58
The Roses of Thought.. 59
The Loud Burst of Uncertainty's Laughter 60
Lines 61
O, Humanity 62
I Am Walking... 63
My Mother... 64
The Nature Around Me... 65
In My Vicinity 66
To the Moon 67
The Great Mountain 68
Silence of the Forest 69
Questions.. 70
To My Neighbor, the Tree 71
Silence... 72
A Story: Samir Was Excited to Death 73
A Short Statement of the Author's Biography and Thought 75

Preface

This book brings together the Arabic translations of pieces of prose and of poetical prose which are either committed or uncommitted to the poetical meters or to rhyme. I started writing these pieces since the early 1960s when I was residing in Al-Tayyiba, my birthplace, and in Jerusalem, as a student at its university, in Yaafaa (Jaffa), as a teacher of Arabic language and literature at the Arab high school. This period lasted for eight years, from 1960 to 1968. I continued writing pieces of prose and poetical prose during my residence for study at the University of Toronto, Canada, from September 1968 to May 1969, then in Philadelphia in the State of Pennsylvania and in the states of New York, Virginia and New Jersey. Then, came the period of my recruitment since January 1980 as a political affairs officer at the Office of the General Assembly of the United Nations in New York City, then as a reporter, editor, reviser and translator of Arabic records of the meetings held by the United Nations General Assembly, the Security Council, the Disarmament Commission, the Committee on the Exercise of the Palestinian People of Their Inalienable Rights. This collection also contains several pieces which were more recently and originally written in English in New York and New Jersey.

The writings record some of my life experiences, including those which I witnessed during the time of my studies in these lands. These writings are the product of the writer's witnessing of events and developments, and a reflection of his interaction with his socio-political setting and his feeling as a Palestinian in West Jerusalem before the June 1967 war, his longing for Palestine as an idea, vision, people and land and the days he spent in it before his travel in September 1968 to Toronto> In these writings are reflected the painful political, social and psychological reality being lived in various quarters in this sacred city. The tragedies being suffered and continue to be suffered by the Arab people are many; such tragedies are unfolding in almost each spot in the Arab homeland, and had their heavy and loathsome nightmare. Should poetry be defined only as the rhythmical writing or speech, that is to say, without rhyme, then rhythmical poetry would be allowed without be rhymed.

Poetry is not rhythmical speech only. Poetical state can be reflected in various forms of language with its various sounds, rhythms and images, and in meanings, sentiments, feelings and inspirations.

Some of these pieces, particularly those which were written in the 1960s, are short. They include ideas which point at, and criticize, the deterioration of the Arab social, political and economic circumstances and conditions. Longing for Palestine and to visit and see its land were intensely pulling and are still pulling the author to hold the pen to pour feelings of alienation and longing for the homeland.

Whereas in quite a considerable number of pieces, the date of writing and the name of the place of writing are provided, such information is lacking with regard to other pieces. The pieces are placed according to the date of their writing in their backward order. Thus, a piece that was written in 2005 is placed before that which was written in 2003. What helped in the following of this order, in spite of the lack of knowledge of the dates of the writing of these pieces, are the life stages of the author, which helped in the approximate determining of the dating of writing.

To avoid falling into confusion, vowel marks for some words are added for some words whose pronunciation lends itself to different readings.

The Arab traditional or classical definition of poetry is the purposefully rhythmical and metrical speech. Hence, poetry in the Arab tradition is called metric speech, which means the use of a certain rhythm in a poetical meter. In the classical structure of the poem, the poem consisted of a number of lines, which can number as many as 5, 30 or even 100, and each of these lines comprised two separate parts, each of the two does have the same number of poetical or rhythmical metrical speech or writing according to the type of the poetical meter.

Besides this classical or traditional form of poetry, for nearly the last century, Arabic poetry was written without sticking to the principle of having certain number, usually from 6 to 10, of poetical speech parts of the metric line. In this relatively, new form of poetry, one can still meet the condition of writing several parts of the rhythmical speech without complying with providing the classical number of the metric speech parts.

A rhyme can consist of one or more than one letter, but usually not more than 3 letters. Obviously, the larger the number of the letters of a rhyme, the more difficult it is the find a fitting rhyme. With a poet's choice of a 'difficult' rhyme, namely, a rhyme consisting of two, three or four letters, he (she) would have limited his expression of his sentiments and feelings, and would have impeded the smoothness and flow of meaning and sentiments, and forced the poet to use of one language form even though the strength of poetical gushing sometimes makes necessary to ignore the poetical form for the sake of preservation of the semantic and emotional flow. When a classical or traditional form of poetry, whose length is, say, one hundred lines, with each line comprising two sections, having an equal number of rhythmical speech and one rhyme for the whole poem is found, such a form should unavoidably had affected the flow of expression of meaning, sentiment and poetical images.

A poet who writes classical rhythmical poetry might have a sense of a strong pride of writing, after making a certain effort, of a classical poem. This poet might be right in this sense of pride. Objectively, he might have been able to write, through poetry with a different number of rhythmical sections in each line, with or without compliance with the need to rhyming, a poem more expressive, with less efforts, of the meanings, feelings and poetical imaging than the classical poem.

One might consider that rhythmical metrical poetry does not deserve making that many efforts and that it would be more useful for readers as well as culture to reduce the restrictions that accompany classical poetry in order to achieve a greater deal of smoothness and flow of meanings and feelings.

Each one has or should have the right to choose the form or structure of writings. No one has the right to impose on others this or that form of writing. One can, and it would be advisable for him to be, critical on the condition that criticism be relevant or, as much as possible, objective. It is incorrect that a literary piece comprising of lines each of which is consisting of a number of rhythmical parts is regarded as a prose poem. It would be correct to call such a piece as a rhythmical piece.

It would be inappropriate to bring the subject of prose poetry or rhythmical poetry into the context of the discussion or debate taking place about the expression of 'modernity' which involves ideological controversies which require much caution. Some call rhythmical poetry as modern poetry. Rhythmical poetry should be regarded as a development on the road to poetical expression without being classified as modern in the ideological sense or the Western context. To describe what is different or new as modern and that it is inspired by Western thought would be stopped. Such a new thing might be stemming from our original Arab soil, drawn from, or responding, to it.

The poet's desire to be emancipated from the rules or maybe fetters of the classical Arab poem is a very important reason for the use of rhythmical poetry or what is called the free poetry. With the writing of this poetry the poet might be more true to himself, less artificial or free from artificiality and more concerned with meaning and with expression of poetry and less careful about decorative language structures, and his imagination might be roaming with more freedom. It is possible to say that those who write free or rhythmical poetry do believe in the utility of the big common creative space.

I would like to thank Hanin Nashif and Ahmad M. Nashef for their contribution to making this typescript ready for publishing.

Taysir N. Nashif
TNNashif@aol.com
Hamilton, NJ
August 1, 2012

Oh, Human Dignity

Oh, human dignity,
Are you destined to be triumphant in the battle
    against gold?
Will you stand out, confident and strong,
    when the armies of power and domination
    rush to try to assassinate you?
Have you narrated the past stories of human pride
    to your enemies?
And the proud angels of the forest,
    can they be your guiding emissaries to
    the city of noise and hurried walking?
Will your space embrace
    the beautiful women who spread the magic light
    in the dark depths of the oceans?
I have the magic moments and the blessed while
    of warming my heart with warmth of your existence,
    as seen in a child's smile of happiness;
    in an orphan being guided by a human being with
    a generous heart in the long-short march of life;
    in the sight of a thankful displaced person,
    who lost his father, mother and memory,
    carrying a loaf of bread given to his empty stomach:
    in the joy of a peasant,
    carrying a basket of barley and love to his awaiting family.

The Vine Tree Is My Home

Our home is a dream of life
Amid the fig and olive trees in the Holy Land.
Our home is warm with flirtatious silvery waves
And the silvery rays of the moon.
Across star-studded skies my soul journeys through the night along unfamiliar,
magic pathways
To virgin worlds, where love, humanity and hope
Are the constant refrain,
Where enmity and selfishness are but a distant memory.
From our home in the Holy Land,
With veneration and submission,
Like the long wait of a lover
At the temple of the heart-chosen beloved,
I hear the solemn voice of the prophets,
As strong as the rumble of thunder,
Sending God's tidings and warnings.
Our home in the Holy Land nestles
Among the dreaming hills, blessed with orange trees.
My being is saturated with the fragrance
Of a yearning for the blossoming of amity
Between peoples.
A story of kindled love between the peasant and the land
These ever-green and naked trees narrate.
The soft, leafy branches shelter the bees on our land
As our warm home has been a refuge
For the faint and the weary.
Snug under the cover of vine leaves is our home.
Through the space created by the dance of the living leaves,
Rays of life penetrate my soul and my beating heart,
Kindling within me the sacred joy of seeing Mother Earth
And imbuing me with overwhelming love,
And letting my hands roam the space
To reach for the grapes to bestow on my children,
Waiting eagerly below with outstretched hands.

New Orleans Is My Home

In the warm tears that the eyes generously gave,
    roamed all colors.
New Orleans is where countless hearts
    met to stem the angry sea.
Mountain-high waves,
    don't you have mercy on the newly-born child,
    on the beautiful mother,
    who is in helpless race with nature's wrath,
    carrying her fading child
    with her thin breast,
    sharing her milk with the children of the deserted neighborhoods.
In Louisiana and Alabama,
    trees and birds are not celebrating their morning sun,
    and nightly moon,
    for the hands of Miriam and John and Jeanette,
    blessed with wheat and bread, are no longer in sight.
Knights of day and of humanity,
    have you seen with your hearts the girl whom,
    in her eyelashes,
    abodes the youth of America.
Have you seen the old man who,
    with the pen of memory,
    painted the future,
    leaning on the goodness of the present past.
My dear people carried on the raging sea,
    I shall not be salvaged by the sighs of the poets,
    on the route to the elevated shore.
With my anxious arms,
    I laid one hundred roses of hope.
A desire drives me to walk on the confident street of rosy and sweet memories,
    in the city of winds and waves and dreams,
    where the lights are dim, but inspire confidence and hope;
    a message do the lights send;

where the leaves have fallen and are adrift in the uproar of rising waves,
and people have trembled,
    but kept the hope candled in the deep corners of the heart.
Heedless I am to the vanity of the persistent flood.
The jazz of hope and humanity soothes the heart.
The sun will not fade away from the heights of my memory.
The moon will continue,
    with its calming rays,
    guide me back to my home;
    this time, to New Orleans.

I Have a Skill

I have the skill of looking at your eyes,
    Where the beauty and warmth.
I have the skill of appreciating the beauty of your dress,
    Which reminds me of the olive trees of my land.
I have the skill of counting the beatings of my heart,
    When you are away,
    And when I am with you.
I see the roses in your eyes,
    And in your smile, I see the dawn of the morning.
In your voice, I hear the melody of lasting tune.
Let me feel the heat of your feelings,
    And the lasting touch of your hand.

Can We Rejoice

Don't I deserve, my friend, your congratulations
that I am today addressing the beautiful peoples
in the far-close corners of the world?!
My rainbow embraces all colors.
My spirit, without the burden of a passport,
travels,
with an innocent sense of security and reassurance,
with no artificial boundaries and walls,
through the universe and beyond.
Let us rejoice, my companion on the road of life,
in our being,
in our time,
a live human link,
connecting between the infinite past and the infinite future;
in our being a connecting point in time,
between the babies' cries still not heard,
and the unborn babies' smiles.
Rejoice in our being of an unexplained idea
between the unraveled secret of the past
and the conscience of the coming unknown.

On You, O, Children of Africa, My Tears I Shed

The thousand motionless eyes set pointedly,
at infinity,
are stronger than the entirety of our existence.
The small debilitated eyes are faster than light,
mightier than the knight,
sharper than the sword,
in invading the hearts,
millions and millions of hearts,
from the dust of Eritrea to the green lands of Mohawk,
and smiling infant lands.
Oh children of the earth,
the brown eyes of the desert have turned to you.
Oh sons and daughters of the soil,
and of apples,
and meat and play lands,
have you turned your heavy ears to the tearing storm
of the empty stomach?
And the grim winds of Africa,
have they whispered to you the untold story of the dying baby,
helplessly roaming,
with her mouth,
in search of life,
the lifeless body of her mother,
martyred by making,
with a believer's courage,
the long, long journey,
to embrace into her trembling thin hands,
the drops of holy sought-after water
for her innocent fading child.
Oh angels of good,
to you,

with insecure hope,
I turn,
seeking to atone for the repugnant long journey of long caravans,
loaded with bleak miseries
of want and thirst and encounter
with the smiling arrogant death.
And, when the father,
with his skinless shape and tearless eyes
—because no tears are there to be shed—
turned, a short while before he entered eternity,
with the open arms of a body
crucified on the stake of life and dignity,
turned to his disappearing,
vanishing family,
what was the message that he was articulating
more than one thousand Ciceros,
to spread what shakes the earth.
And when the mother,
with her milkless breasts
learned,
before the last departure of her tongueless son,
what was the message that should,
like one million tidings,
have moved the human conscience to
harvest the blessings of wheat,
and to fill the basket of bread from the neighbor.
When the vanishing child's extended arms
were withdrawn with a weak human sigh,
for there was no loaf for parents' loafless hands
to fill the child's revolting being,
a magnificent celebration of contented malice,
by the evil creatures of night,
was heard in the specious stretches
of the land.
Your eyes,
oh Mamadou,
are steadier than the mountain,
if only the clear light of humanity has removed the

deluding myth of mocking boundaries.
And your tears,
oh Safiyah,
are heavier and more precious
than tons of barley and corn,
if only the beauty of men and women on the snow
and on the mountains had discovered Safiyah
with her God-given beauty in the
waterless desert and the green watery forests.
Where is the knight who,
with one giant strike and an
all-embracing power,
ended the dreaded evils.
Where is the selfless man,
Whose blessed stride was spacious,
spaceless, embracing stretches of the earth,
from the land of poverty to the land of plenty.
Where is the hero who,
in the blink of an eye, delivered to the peoples of the desert
the tidings of life and the rays of a smile.
Where is the mother of the earth who,
With her rich and generous breasts,
Overwhelmed her sons and daughters
with the blessed sanctified milk?
Where is the sheriff who,
With a sensitive humanity like a
nourishing healing summer wind,
spread out,
like the deed of a magician,
the salvaging straw,
to which clung,
with their soft pure hands,
all the life-thirsty children?
Where is the messenger,
whose message has no color,
whose word is the word of race-less humanity
of fellow-citizenship of
this one, shared small flying star?

Tears Are Falling on Humanity

I am out of the familiar.
To keep to the familiar puts me in prison, and I want to be free.
With thought and emotion, I stand in the swirl of the current,
or on its bank, because the current is part of the familiar.
I stand in the swirl of the current and I see other currents
running in different directions.
I walk along the bank of the gushing river,
my emotions with rivers in my conscience running towards other worlds.
A house with foundations cemented from the tears of the miserable and
   the suffering of the deprived is not a home for me.
I shall not smell the fragrance of the jasmine in a place whose corners
   were founded on the sweat of the exhausted, the tired and the weak.
A dwelling place for the slave women, carriers of the fans for the prince
   to satisfy his ego, is not part of my valuables.
I do not know to draw the image of the ruler.
I have no painting of the pasha.
These figures have no room in my memory.

My Homeland

O, my homeland,
I yearn for you as a rain cloud which quenches my thirsty self,
    and the miserable hills.
I long for you as a sea in which my bewildered sail surges.
      as a river in which my self's stretching shadows slumber,
      as an address for my alienated name.
I stare at you as a memory of my history which is scented with
    tragedies and storms.
The sadness will not suppress the voice of my miserable people.
The star of night narrates their story.
The pains of my people are rising on the top of the mountains.
The orchard of my land is a fragrance on my mind.
Your bright dawn intoxicates the viewer.

With My Pen
I have Fenced-In My Garden

My pen is my unknown world.
On my letters, my yearnings are flooding.
My pen is a shield for my identity and myself.
The walls of my castle were drawn with my writings.
With my castle, I am protecting my freedom.
With my pen, I hedged in my garden.
In my garden, frankness takes sway.
From snow, I go to the warmth of past years.
My pen narrates the story of slumbering hills.
My pen moves on the rhythm of the moon.
The moon passes the night with those who love nightly chat.
I am singing for the night, the forest and the trees.
'Ibaal has drawn in me the grooves of the homeland.
My yearnings got me excited to see our green fields.

My Brother, Don't Deny Me the Warmth of Humanity

My vocabulary is free from the restrictions of "I" and "they."
Humanity is my code of guidance.
Through humanity we are liberated from biases and intolerance.
My address is a home that stretches across the blue waters, from the
    Caribbean to Hawaii, and from Tahiti to the Mediterranean.
My address is the earth with its beautiful colors and seasons.
There are no colors in my memory and humanity.
White for me is the color of snow,
of rice for the poor, of glowing waves of sunshine for human warmth.
Black is the color of nature when it covers lovers with the warmth of
    privacy of love.
Compassion and love are the roads leading to my home.
God bless all peoples, all mankind.
With God's all-embracing mercy and guidance, we are all the chosen
    creatures of God.
With love and humanity, a rope of brotherhood and sisterhood unites
    my heart with all the miserable people on Earth.
The human creature born in Timbuktu I call him the brother from
    poverty-stricken Africa.
I swear to you, my brother, from far continents and different cultures,
by the prophets in whom you and I believe, I am looking for humanity,
to salvage us from the whims of ourselves.
It may be a source of joy for you, my misguided brother, to see all the
    evils in me.
Maybe this makes you feel you are superior.
You will not subdue humanity in me.
Let us learn the wisdom of the sages, who tell us the stories of man's
    miseries.
With my love, in support of humanity, your heart will be cleansed
    from the evil ignorance of beautiful humanity; it will free you from

the bondage of bias and restore to you the immortal kingdom of
humanity.

For my living and sustenance, it is sufficient for me to fill the stomach
with barley bread and olives.

I can survive on a half-empty stomach.

My stomach, lungs and soul I know to satiate with the fragrance of
orange and lemon and apple from the Holy Land,

on Earth and in my soul.

My brother, do not burn, with your fire, the orchards, so that all of us be
sheltered under our mother's green love and protection.

Don't, my brother, harshly treat the oceans, for they, with their human
experiences, tell the immortal story of humanity.

One person lost is one too many.

Let, then, humanity, with one concerted humble song, sing in all corners
of the small Earth.

With our vulnerabilities and weaknesses we are equal.

The dictionary of my mind is devoid of the unfamiliar word of
superiority over my neighbors in the other continents beyond the
connecting seas.

I left a share of dates and dry bread for your empty stomach, my brother.

This is the only food I have to share with you.

I do not lie down to rest, over-stuffed with food much needed by the
poor and miserable of generous Earth.

I have conscience qualms over the over-consumed dwindling resources
of our over-milked mother Earth.

It is inhuman that you do not sense my humanity, brother.

You have no right to deny me the warm shelter of humanity.

The oil of Divinity has blessedly covered my Earth-colored skin.

My breath is permeated with the spirit of the immortal to which both
you and I belong.

Where are the angels of good who come forth to salvage humanity from
the overwhelming whim of unsatisfied desire?

Where are the knights of good tidings who remove the thorns from
the one road of humanity to a world free from myths of divided
humanity?

A world where the clasped hands of the east and west form an elevated
bridge to humanity in its happy march to self-assurance and peace
on Earth.

Come

Come to watch the birds,
carrying on their back the blue-purple space,
to look attentively at the vibrating water waves
that were caused by the beaks of the birds,
seeing their shadows in the clarity of the spring waters,
and to listen to the tunes of the valley,
whose trees and forests
water the stories of the by-gone generations,
and whose brides dance magically on the melodies of sunset,
which is drawing close to the earth
and promptly surrounds it with its covers,
at mid-night,
and before the early signs of the coming of the new dawn.
Accompany me, my brother,
For I have loathed emptiness.

Deep Sadness

These my days, my school,
made me trembling.
I am still in the hands of sorrow;
Under the fist of the pressing time.
I am consoled by my accompanying sweet sadness.
I am saturated with the flames of the lost childhood dreams.
And, when I head for the mature garden,
with its whispering trees,
and my sight stretches to the far extents of the great sea,
the self is relieved with the aromatic plants and ambergris trees.

Our Feet Are Bleeding

We were young.
We picked flowers on the sides of the roads.
In our hearts we watered the roses.
Love spread warmth in the heart.
The sun accompanied us to our dreaming villages.
From the midst of the dark clouds,
sunshine appeared.
After long days, our feet are bleeding
from the thorns of the road.
On the shoulders there are burdens of the times.

A Raven of Separation

The raven of separation is croaking.
It watches all the doings of my people from the world of sadness.
Because of the raven,
my stretching branches have fallen,
and my large trees with the shadowy leaves.
From the east and the west,
the raven of separation flapped its wings.
With its croaking, security and tranquility in
our non-existence disappeared.

The Clusters of My Grape Garden Are Generous

The clusters of my grapes garden are generous.
Its branches are soaring in my free imagination.
I trampled on my grapes and dreams.
Today, I am wandering.
In the unpleasant wonders of the world,
my roads are lost.
Why my immortal river has dried up,
when I am looking for my boat?
When the sun of my garden will rise?
Then, I will enjoy the shadows with modesty.

Marching to the Hill of Virtue

I am carrying the heart to there,
where the hill of virtue exists.
I am walking.
I run, then fall forward,
then, I continue running; then, I fall forward.
This is my permanent road.
My heart is vitalized with dreams.
Good is my constant desire.

Let Us Be Free

Come, let us start off, o, my lover, to the fields,
as nature has smiled,
the evergreen cypress is dressed with beauty,
and spring has surrounded the mountains with
its green arms in warmth and elation.
Come, so that we start off, my companion, to the forest,
to listen to the whisper of the brooks,
the song of the evergreen oak,
the hymn of the blackbird,
and to the stories of the former residents of the quarter,
narrated by their beautiful homes and roads.
Kiss me, my lover, as the sun is blessing me with its touch;
embrace me, as the forest is embracing me;
and smile at me, as the daisy is smiling at me.
The tunes of the flute brought back to me the stories of past generations.
They drive away sadness from the heart.
They move loneliness far away from the self.
Do you hear, as I do, the choir of angels,
Repeating, in the limitless space,
The melody of nature?
Do you feel, as I do, the Divine Spirit in the space of this blessed earth?
Look at the flying birds with their eyes filled with tears
for the sun sinking into the ocean>
O, birds, the encroachment of night on day grieves you.
The cold of gloom carries away your wishes.
Did your lovers desert you at sunset?
The visions of the vague night horrify you.
Have you felt a tricky night?
A dawn of a new day will rise.
The birds will be back to kiss the virgin violet.
Tomorrow, the tears of narcissus will spread hope in the heart.
The lips of roses will open up for a new love.
The nightingale will repeat the song of the brook.

The dreams of the forest will be spread by the innocent sparrows from remote spaces.
Together we shall repeat, with the warmth of belief, the prayer to the Great and Beautiful Entity.

Freedom

No freedom without equality.
Freedom means responsibility.
Enslavement is theft.
Chaos is not freedom.
It is slave's right to emancipate himself.
Captivity can make the human being a captive,
but it does not necessarily make him a slave.
Freedom is not donated as a gift to the human being.
It is taken, not given.
Human being cannot be liberated but through his power.
Freedom is a thing that is sought by a reasoning man.

A Song for Peace in the Holy Land

May peace lighten our hearts, children of Abraham,
children of Adam.
May peace prevail, where bloodshed has long reigned, hatred in the
     domain of oblivion.
May all the children of Adam and Eve,
share the warmth of happiness and the moon-like tranquility of
     assurance,
free from the shackles of anxiety and the repulse of fear,
where the mind and the heart have become questing eyes,
to see justice for all the tired but yearning humane brothers and sisters,
where grandfathers and grandmothers,
pregnant with stories of thorns and tortured tears, loudly declare to the
     grandson,
with great determination,
the brave humanizing story of peace,
whose golden pages stretch from our mother earth to the watching
     heavens,
whose enduring letters,
like a true love story,
with penetrating rays of daring hope were written.
May peace be there,
where tanks have become tractors,
and rifles have become stalks,
on which vine leaves grow,
with whose juice the triumph of peace we shall perpetually celebrate,
where men no longer talk the language of war,
where the battle whinnying of horses gives way,
as wide as the earth,
to the kisses of love,
and red rose-carrying palms.
Let the message conceived in the heart of the Holy Land,
digested in the minds of men and women,
with a fainting hope,

24

stamped in the hearts of the fatherless, of the widows, be one of justice,
  of mutual love,
and human dignity for all the creatures of God,
with their different but beautiful colors of skin and eyes and hair.
Let that message,
stronger than one million strong, and one thousand tanks,
and more enduring than gold and steel,
let that powerful message shine on me and us and you.
Let that message, with its irresistible force,
with its glowing letters of the ink of history,
reverberate now and forever more.
Let the ink of history,
with its myriad of outstretched arms,
as long as a journey of hope and wait of a lover,
and with its beseeching and appealing eyes,
sow the seeds of barley,
with whose fruit to drink the toast of peace,
and grow the young fig trees, vines and olives,
in each village and town and home,
with their green leaves announcing to all,
from east to west,
the onrush of the long-awaited spring of life.
Let that message, with its blessings,
overwhelm each grain of sand,
on whose shores, swimmers have but the soothing waves of fear-free joy.
Let its spirit travel high, high, to the skies,
and to the stars,
so that the earthly creatures bring the tidings to
the heavens that humanity on earth has prevailed,
and that we sure deserve the God's blessings.

To Humanity

Philadelphia, PA
December 1969

You are a source of anxious yearnings.
Your olive forest is saddened
that helpless, confused and bewildered people
do not turn to you.
How much beautiful that the human
being settles in the nest of your soft and warm branches.
Your vitality sends out vitality to me.
Your nature is superabundant, unending.
Your distances are unlimited.
They are not approached by people oblivious to you,
unaware of themselves,
those who are naively indulging in the oblivion of their seconds,
and are forgetting their mother.
You are their mother.
You shelter them because you are generous and spacious.
You embrace them because all of you is goodness and generosity.

To the Forest

Look, the moon has risen, and with it
hills have been unified by their summits.
The summits of the tall trees
floated in the flowing light.
Come, then, with me to the flowing creek,
to accompany it to the sea.
Let us go to the lovely slopes,
as the evergreen cypress is still swinging on the rhythm
of the breeze.
Come with me, my brother, to the forest,
the simple, the modest,
in order for it to give us beauty from
its beauty and strength from its strength.
Don't you want to listen to the whispers of the birds?!
With their assurance of the ages
And affectionate memories, you will feel their echoes
in the depths of your bewildered self.
Don't you want to watch the clouds,
while carrying the space on their back!?
Then, they take it away from the noise of the city.

Waves Have Not Drowned My Small Boat

My friend,
trust that I exist.
Days have not slain my big heart.
My sadness has not shattered my beautiful dreams.
Waves have not drowned my small boat.

Trees of Evergreen Cypress

Toronto

The trees of the evergreen cypress are tall.
They have only one road:
They accompany the clouds in the free space.
The towering trees of the evergreen cypress are
embraced by the rays of the sun,
and kissed by the winds.
They are warm.
Rain draws its badge of honor on the trees.
Evergreen cypress trees vie with mountains in their loftiness.
They stare at the stars and the moon.
Grasses are protected with their shadows.
Birds, fleeing the cold, find refuge in their breath.
The tall, lofty and towering trees are closer to the skies.
They overlook on the lands.
And spread their shadows on the mountains, plains and the sea.
Evergreen cypress trees are modest, though tall.
Their origin is in the land.
They are strong and proud.
They protect the pigeons and the swallow,
with their wings telling the coming of spring.

Your Big Sea of Love

Toronto, 1969

In your big sea of love,
I am a wandering boat.
In your dreaming love,
Flows the triumph of youth.
Hadn't been for you,
I wouldn't have roamed the wider space.
In the world of your vibrant breath,
my wide horizons are glowing.

Calm of the Sea

Toronto, January 1969

Calmness of the sea,
you will not reach its depths.
Calmness of the sea,
its waves ridiculed the inability of the divers
to comprehend its contents.
To the sands that are slumbering on the
Warmth of the sun returns the sailor exhausted,
while the sea is in its quiet.
I am in the heart of the night
On the shore of the great sea,
While my self is wrapped with spacious darkness.

Melting the Ice

Toronto, January 3, 1969

I am looking for a heater,
on which to hang this heart,
that cannot escape from residing in my interior.
Perhaps warmth can melt its ice,
on the deep tone of a robust ance.

Peace of Mind

February 13, 1969

Peace of mind,
I have heard of it,
but I haven't found it.
It is in a place whose name I know not.
Peace of mind,
is it residing in a non-landing island
to which a boat will not go.
It may be in a forest
whose tall trees with many branches I have not seen.
Peace of mind,
may be abiding in a hut, whose form I do not know.
Peace of mind,
mankind has not seen
in the quiet of the night,
and the broad daylight.

Tranquility of Nature

Blend of the human spirit with the spirit of nature leads to truth.
Fragrance of the rose sends to the self lover for the creator and for
    humanity.
The road to the forest is the road to truth.
The human being says:
I shall build a house in the sky.
With its air is of humanity.
Its doors are of freedom.
Its windows are of equality.
Its walls are of fraternity.
Its foundations are of justice.
Its pillars are of love, and its dwellers are humane.

My Writing Pen Cannot Draw My Image

Toronto, January 23, 1969

At night,
in the light of a candle,
I am listening to silence.
Into existence my existence dives.
My life is hills, plains and valleys,
flowing breezes,
heaving storms,
sweet creeks,
limitless oceans.
My writing pen cannot move
to quickly draw my image.

A Kiss in the Dark

Toronto, January 8, 1969

In the deep darkness,
my spirit is a torch.
My spirit is a candle with abiding light.
It gives light for you.
In the deep darkness,
there is an abundant calm.
In a long, long hour,
on the peak of our night,
a kiss flourished.
An assertive lighting candle
lights for you and for me the path,
leading to an unknown journey.

Days Have Gone By

Toronto, January 8, 1969

Days have gone by without slackening.
My soul yearns to freedom,
To a world shadowed with amity and love.
Is our life a piece of ice?
One day the ice will melt into water.
Days have passed.
They faded away anxiously like mirage,
behind dunes of the time.
In my face, the garden will not flourish
For me the birds will not sing in the chasm of space.
I was a youngster.
I gazed at the sun,
in the morning, at noon and sunset.
In the waves of rays and wishes, my arms were open for pleasure.
Into the waves, my soul was submerged.
My wishes I cultivated in my wide spaces.
Olive trees and the old homes are the fragrance of my dreams.
With tolerance I watered my garden.
My garden was wrapped with the rains of my spring.
My forest was wide.
To it came every displaced.
My forest was overflowing with its tenderness.
Then, I was a youngster.
Years, without bidding farewell, have faded away.

Wails of Humanity

Toronto, January 5, 1969

Oh, what a malicious pleasure of evil!
Oh, what a quarrelsome noise of gloom!
Piles of ice are present in front of me.
They overlook with their head like snales.
Do you, my self, listen
to the wails of humanity?
And to the wails of its tears?
Are you falling to the chasms of non-existence?
From the East spread a great melody.
Save, o, you, mankind.
I am your brother.
Are you doubting that?!
Dreeam was tickled by the flowers of the homeland.
Our waters are your waters from the tears of the sky.
I am from your kind.
I was not deprived of my mother's compassion.
In her heart, there is room for you also.
This, my hand, is stretched out to you.
My hand is relaxing.
Shake my hand.
Don't let down humanity.

Emptiness

Toronto, January 3, 1969

Sometimes, I sit in such a way,
with no purpose.
Sometimes, I dive into the space and the sea.
Winds on me blow.
I chew my emptiness.
And different self conditions,
Compete with each other.
Among people I have sowed my seeds.
What is the fate of my seeds?
Will they grow in a favorable climate?
Will the freeze kill them?
Will they perish from the over-heat?
I again chew my thirst.
Then, I look at the distances,
filled with empty spaces.
Then, I bid farewell to the ending day.

My Sense of Humanity Is Stronger

Toronto, October 22, 1968

No, you, ignorant of humanity,
you will not be able to destroy my humanity.
My sense of humanity is stronger than your ignorance of humanity.
You will not have the upper hand by making me hate you
because of the lack of your humanity, as it does not know hatred.
I will not hate you, as my humanity is strong.
My humanity is wide, inclusive and global.
It accommodates the overlooking and forgetting of your humanity.
You are ethically poor,
and my humanity taught me to be compassionate towards the poor.
You are weak, and my humanity makes me
kind to the weak.
Your world is arid, but the drops of my rain reach it.
They grow roses and narcissus.
How rich my humanity is!
It distributes to you forgiveness for you.

The Great Sea

1968

From the inspiration of your tunes, o sea,
I find my road to infinity.
From the songs of your waves,
I set out to the unknown worlds.
With my strength drawn from your magic and beauty,
I stand in the midst of the hurricanes.
Your blueness, o, sea,
paints my life with joy,
enriches my existence with affection,
and colors my own gardens with elation.
You are my companion in my loneliness.
Your neighborhood consoles me in my gloom.
Your vitality resembles that of a child being carried by the mother.
From yourself you draw strength and significance.
Your dimensions captivate me with their infinity.
The meanings which are inspired by your being
open and closed are the meanings of your greatness.
Your stretching-out extensions cover many hidden worlds.
I smile with innocence at your summer waves on your chest.
And, in front of your winter's wrath,
I stand humbly,
acknowledging the great need for you.

The Great Shore of Jaffa

Dying-down lamp lights are swimming in corridors of misery.
Wooden boats are fettered by human hands.
Warm sails are planted in the water.
They do not traverse the sea of rescue.
A sea is there.
My sea is there.
With me it exchanges yearning.
Jaffa's gulf is generous.
The grateful heart is open for this weeping sea.
I am conscious of it from long, long time ago.
It is warmth of the heart with my dream.
It embraces the lands of Jaffa from the storm.
O, the gulf of my waiting country,
on your bottom are echoes of the songs and nights.
You are remaining forever,
in spite of the marks of the times.

To the Sea of Jaffa

Jaffa, June 14, 1966

Oh, I wish my parts were distributed to you,
o, sea.
This is my great wish.
Your constant movement expresses great meanings.
Because I am part of your existence,
you are part of me.
Your resolve is unlimited.
The ships that your waters carry are but human vanity.
Ships on your waters are proud because
they do not know your strength.
But you are great and infinite in your meaning and significance.
Oh, you, the great sea,
how much myself loves you.
In you are the qualities of humanity and greatness,
because you are humble.
The diamonds of your waters embrace
the humans, and have fun with children.
I shall not desert you in spite of the circumstances of the world,
because you taught me to be strong with you.
In the evening,
I pray with you,
o, great sea,
prayer of the self.
And before sunset,
when I return tired to you,
o, great sea,
you generate in me strength, hope and yearnings,
that overwhelm my existence,
and then make me aspire to emancipation to your existence.

Traversing the Desert

It was written while in the bus to Jaffa, June 1966

A gloomy sky.
Trees are permeated by nature.
A self is pondering for long the secret of existence.
I experience the breeze of my tender self.
My self flows as a river of clouds.
My God, I am traversing the distant deserts of the space.
I hover in a paradise of yearning.
Is this the myth of my paradise?
In between my two wings beats my innocent heart.
I live on the visions that resemble a solemn human gleam of light.
In myself there are thick forests of nostalgia.
In it, relentless hesitation is blended in the past of my exiled life.

At Sunset

1966

You, o, mountains, are the glory of God.
On you is reflected the greatness of the Creator.
You are the lasting song of God.
Your existence provides us with confidence in whatever is around us.
Your steadiness gives us a strong belief.
Through you, I see immortality.
While contemplating your peaks, I understand nature.
Your tunes create tranquility within me.
Your singing brings about calm and peace in my heart.
You are a lasting concrete idea.
The horizon with its wings is swallowed by darkness.
Directions are confused and gushing forth in the approaching night.
The whale of the night will soon swallow the space.
The falling horizon lights are bidding good-bye to the departing day.
The self is stretching itself to the distances.
It is disgruntled when hearing the ambiguous boisterous laughter
of the night, absorbed in heavy worries,
and shaken by pale ideas.
They seem they are coming from volcanic bursts.
The self wants to be emancipated,
to spaces unlimited by gloomy horizons.
To where are you marching, o, sad self?
Are you determining my fate?
Do you aspire to a safer and better world?
You shun injustice on earth.
Courageous are you, my self.
You are not fearful of mounting the unknown sea.
Great are you, myself.
You are roaming the infinite space.
You are striving to identify your place under the sun,
so that you set out, afterwards, to freedom.

I Stood, Looking Out

I stood in the front of my window,
while the full moon looking out at your bedchamber.
Your memory is strong, o, dear.
For me, you are the princess of the land,
and a pearl of the seas.

O, Myself

O, myself,
why are you driving your clouds to the rocky lands,
whereas the rocky lands grow no flowers?
For what are you seeking to grow roses in the deserts,
whereas deserts lack drops of rain?
Why are you leading yur armies to battle the waves of the ocean,
whereas the storms of the ocean are stubborn, o myself?

My Being

In the train from Jaffa to Jerusalem
June 1966

Is there no escape from myself?
I revolt against myself and against many things.
Whatever a journey of life is there,
let me, o self, live.
My yearning revolts against your fetters.
It threatens to undermine the pillars of your torture.
I shall trample down my deep wounds.
Come with me,
your loneliness has affected you,
in the desert of your world with its leafless trees.
Come with me, so that we
sing the songs of the flock on the slope of our youth.
Come with me,
so that we overlook the clashing waves of our sea.

Uncertainty of the Self

March 5, 1965

Silence is pulling me forcibly to every side.
Around me are dancing generations of the past and the present.
Ideas and memories are surrounding me.
Am I uncertain, led by ideas on the long road,
to where I do not know?!
Questioning is hovering above me,
which has no color,
from the depth of myself where my feelings and ideas
are clashing with each other.
I dare to try to fathom the depths of myself.
Questioning of existence accompany me during my journey.
In myself, I came across sands and shades.
My self is leading me to worlds of thick vagueness,
and of a blend of mirage and hope.

The Mother

Jerusalem, January 1965

My mother,
how much I love you, my mother.
You are virtuous, an angel.
You are my example in my life.
You are a lasting light,
a torch of an unending life.
Your big heart overflows with compassion,
and replete with affection.
You are always my refuge in my distress.
How much pleasant I find this heavenly word.
You are my source of help in times of hardships,
a spring of goodness and love.
You are humanity,
embodied in your compassion, love and affection.
Your care, my mother, is always the song on my tongue,
and is the pulse of my heart.
O you pure, noble and strong,
my mother.
Your sweet smile spreads light in my heart.
Your image fills my existence,
and charges me with hope because you are my consolation.
Your smile spreads calm in my depths,
and tranquility in myself.
With seeing you, my heart dances with interior rejoice.
With meeting you, I am pleased and blessed.
How much I wish to meet you to shower you with kisses on your face.
I imagine you in my mind in the morning and the evening,
in the bright day and in the quiet night,
in the early morning and at sunset.
You hugged me when I was young,
and surrounded me with your compassion when I am grown up.

With you I am rich.
Your treasure is overflowing with love.
I shall not find a substitute for you.
With your innocence you are strong,
stronger than the knights.
Time has not subdued you.
Calamities of time have not affected your super-humanity.
Your belief is an inexhaustible fortune.
In me you have planted ambition.
You are my consolation in my distress.

Love of Nature

Jerusalem, 1965

O nature,
O mother, the source of affection.
O my beloved,
I whisper into your depths.
I seek your haven, O my refuge always,
in my adversity and in my tranquility.
Salvage the human beings from thirst,
and save miserable people from hunger and want.
Ward off my brothers in humanity
grief of deprivation and exile.
You are my mother, surrounding me with your consoling arms.
Your lights are my guidance in my life journey.
Your quite waves take me sailing to magical seas.
Your mountains lead me to security and tranquility.
You are my mother,
and I love you so much.

My Young Woman
Is Dancing for the Moon

Jerusalem 1965

My young woman is dancing for the moon,
under the trees,
embracing sweet basil and ambergris.
My young woman is wearing green dress,
on the threshing floor,
chatting in the evening with the innocent date palms,
and spending the night with the stars.
My young women is a butterfly amidst the flowers,
toying with the young goat of our neighbor,
at the water spring of our quarter.
My young woman sings for the brook,
diving into the Mediterranean sea,
looking at the dreaming young man,
sinking into a revolting silence,
in the shadow of the pine trees and the ambergris.
My young woman,
how beautiful is my young woman.
She embraces the rising dawn.
My dreams swim shining,
striding in waves of nostalgia and expectation.

My Beloved

1965

You have, my beloved, a child's smile which I love,
because it reflects a human happiness.
Do butterflies still visit you with their golden wings.
Your look is an immortal story.
You are an example for my imagination.
My overburdened thought is wandering around,
looking for a resting place.
Is there a resting place?
Against myself my thought is revolting.
Questioning is within me.
To where is the journey?
For what is the journey?
Deserts of existence are so extensive.
In them are sands, storms and volcanoes.
In them is a deep mirage.
But, I shall continue the journey,
with my small heart, with my big heart.

The Home and the Olive Tree

I am spending the night with the stars.
I am listening to whispers of silence,
under cover of night.
For them, the strings of the heart were deeply touched.
I am flamed with thought.
To the distant mother I am yearning,
and to my deserted home,
my green garden,
dancing with the moon.
My old olive tree is growing upright with the greatest pride.
In front of them are passing the processions of the humble generations.

Autumn of the Hearts

1965

My woe unto the people.
Their hearts are enveloped with autumn,
and their passion is covered with ice.
Worries surround their feelings.
Doubt colors their view.
And their days are covered with the
color-less memory with dusty features.

O Moon

Tower Street, Jerusalem
April 1965

O moon,
are you smiling to us in humility in spite of your sublimity?
Are you mocking the human affairs with pride?
You perhaps are watching closely and quietly all of our doings.
Are you narrating to us the story of the people who are no
longer residing on these mountains?
What is your direction, o shining moon?
Are you moving towards a lover of yours who is awaiting you?
Or, are you moving towards a place where you hide from
the evils on the earth?
Is your journeying exhausting you, leading
you to desire to quiet, far away from man's coveting of your beauty?
Has my people's deep moaning strengthened your resolve to disperse the
darkness?

Loss of the Oases

The thick covers of my forgetting wipe out
my strayed oases in the deserts of time.
Collapsing dusty walls are surrounding me.
From the corners of the deep past,
I am surrounded by fog with a raven's color and depth of night.
This fog increases uncertainty.
My beloved, you are missed.
In my memory are the nights of chestnut.
Where is the radiant rosy garden and forest,
under whose stretching branches,
shadows were sought which gave refuge with tranquility.

The Roses of Thought

Tayyibih, April 1965

With their fragrance, roses immerse me.
How generous the roses are.
Their glowing face is beating with life.
Your existence, oh, roses, is cloaked with purity.
Your entity spreads a heavenly aroma.
You are worlds of a lasting light.
Because you are confident in sunrise,
you give us belief in life,
Silence around me is listening to the tunes of your melodies.
The waves of your colors are spreading joy in the mind.
Your spirit permeates each grain of land, oh, roses.
You are a rhymed and rhythmical poem.
With my eyes, I embrace you.
With the glare of your beauty, you are embracing me.
Your dance melts the ice of my past;
then, it becomes a time space of comfort.
The eyes find warmth with landing on your chest.
Thus, the ice of the heart turns into rain that flows
with the singing creeks hurrying to the deep seas.
When the morning rays kiss you, my dreams flow as flowers.
It is so inspiring that I and you belong to one land.
Looking at you floods my mind with songs,
and makes the sources of life flow in my entity.
You are the source of my inspiration,
and the origin of my giving.

The Loud Burst of Uncertainty's Laughter

Al-Qatamon, Jerusalem
March 13, 1965

Uncertainty is moving wildly in the depths.
The waves of memory are pushing one another.
Is the earth falling down to the deep abyss?
Am I suffering from standing in front of the unknown,
or am I appearing in front of destiny?
Specters crowding the space with their breath shake silence.
The smile is fading away.
A rose that dawns in my past is withering.
It is, then, crushed by the sands of my life.
From far I hear the drums of ugly emptiness.

Lines

The University, Jerusalem
July 27, 1964

Nature embraces me with its smooth arms,
like a tenderhearted mother.
Forest hugs me to its pure chest,
like a lover.
The lofty mountains of eternity,
are rushing to meet the moving summer clouds,
shelter me with their attending tranquility,
as the moon light takes soothing care of the
miserable hungry people of our planet.
The evening breezes of beautiful Jerusalem,
with its many rose-smelling quarters,
and with its magical fingertips,
engage my thought and feelings.
They make me lift my face up towards infinity.
A deep silence overwhelmes my existence.
Mount Scopus, immortally existing there,
salvages me from the silence.
Night enwraps me with its love,
as the immortal virgins of the sea enwrap
the young humanity covering,
with extended arms and open palms pointing up to the skies,
the soft chest of our mother Earth.

O, Humanity

How much do I need to set out in the shadow
of your overwhelming light,
and to dive into your infinite depths.
Great are you, o, humanity.
You resemble the sun.
With your pure lights,
the depths of human beings are shining.
I see nothing that equal humanity's presence in our material existence.
Your file is filled with sublime values and principles.
How strong is my elation for you.
I prostrate in deference at your feet.
Out of love for you, I bend my head.
Your meaning is freedom.
Thus, grant me freedom and grant me life.
I seek your protection.
You make me secure from fear.
You are a divine manifestation.

I Am Walking

My heart is beating with tears over humanity.
Sometimes, my heart is revolting against a world witnessing commission
    of evils.
I am walking and keep walking.
To where I am walking?
Is there a road?
Life my heart wants,
with tranquility as its space,
with light overwhelming the horizons of tranquility,
with life founded on mercy and virtue.
Where is life and where is virtue?!
But, I am still walking, without arrival.

My Mother

My mother is the inspiration of my dreams.
She is the holy source of maternal love,
and the deep poetic ring.
My mother is a lasting warm smile.
She is the pulse of the strong yearning,
fragrance of jasmine,
and a rose kissed by eternity.
My mother is a melody of the seasons,
and a tune of nature.

The Nature Around Me

Jerusalem, May 8, 1964

How much a pure and generous mother are you.
Your heart is overflowing with compassion on your children.
You are flowing with beauty and splendor.
I kneel down to your throne of your mercy.
I prostrate myself before your beauty and strength.
O mother, I am part of you.
I shall remain fascinated by your generosity.
I am overjoyed by the heavenly tones of your strings,
and the songs of your immortality.
My beloved,
you are a song in the waves of your breath and immortality,
and as a hymn in the throne of your magnificence.

In My Vicinity

Allenby Camp, Baq'a, Jerusalem
July 15, 1964

You are a smile on the face of time,
and a reflection of light in the darkness in the world.
A star is our neighbor.
It shared nature with both of us
and witnessed our presence.
I feel jealousy from it of you.
My darling, you are the moving song of nature.
You are the lyrical string of immortality,
and a magical song wrapped by the
universe with an enduring smile of yearning.
How beautiful is the glow of your ambitious eyes.

To the Moon

Jerusalem, March 25, 1964

You are moving on rhythmically among the stars,
and in nature,
free, towering and lofty.
My self is watching and guarding you,
and the beloved nature.

The Great Mountain

7 Tower Street, Jerusalem

I looked at you, oh, the great mountain,
seeing in you myself.
I looked at your high slopes,
seeing my face reflecting them.
Oh, what an immortal mountain with your steadiness,
as the immortality of humanity.
The tree of pine nut in your bosom is an idea of existence.
How often I secluded myself with you!
How much beautiful was my seclusion!
How often the town became too narrow for me!
Consequently, you became my refuge.
You are my confidant; you listened to me.
With gentleness and compassion,
I took good care of your roses,
Causing me to be in good spirits.
Oh, the song of the radiant nature.
Oh, the melody of the skies.
Oh, the steady and proud entity.
Because I am part of you,
I shall not be far from you and your shadow.
You are my refuge in distress.

Silence of the Forest

Jerusalem, 1961

How beautiful is listening to silence of the forest stretching very far,

and the breezes, moving the tops of the serene trees, with the trees
covered with green.

The more listening you show, the greater is your enjoyment of the
presence of the ingenious immortal nature.

Forest, with its meanings, prevails over your existence. Thus, you cannot
but venerate it and prostrate for its beauty which is reaching the
peak of perfection.

Forest contains meanings that books do not contain.

Contemplate, my brother, nature, while rains return to its bosom and
overwhelm it with kisses.

Come with me, my brother, to accompany the brook flowing in the
heart of the forest.

Come, so that nature gives us the blessings of its spirit.

Join me to the strong and modest, beautiful and genuine, simple and
pure nature. Come on to the hills, bending to the wide slopes
interacting with the magical rays of the sun.

Questions

1960

Limitless thick darkness hovers around me.
Ghosts are wildly roaming and leaping,
as if they are engaged in a battle with nothing,
while I am chewing my straying colorless
and vague thought and concerns.
Almost bursting silence shrouds my room.
Tumult rages in my depths,
the whle of me . . .
But who am "I"?
Where am "I"?
What is "where"?
What is "what"?
What is the question?
What is the answer?
What is "truth," what is existence?

To My Neighbor, the Tree

Naked as my soul,
in days of autumn,
are you.
Through you, silence has spread,
O my neighbor.
Are you waiting for the awakening of spring?
Your leaves, as a crown of glory,
have disappeared.
Shall they return, with the return of the birds,
yearning for their warm nests?
Shall yearning in my heart,
which got bored of apathy, return?!

Silence

Silence is roaming in my room.
Bewilderment about the seemingly life contrasts
is overwhelming me.
Darkness is surrounded by discontent around me.
Cosmos is my home.
A glowing star, far close, is my companion in my journey.
It is sadly looking down upon me.

A Story:
Samir Was Excited to Death

Samir, who was 20 years old, hardly believed that the dream which for a long time had spurred his imagination had at last been realized. The smile quickly returned to his mother's face after it had departed following the sudden passing away of Samir's brother for an unknown reason. Samir's father said—as a deep sadness appeared on his face—that once he took Samir to a physician residing in a town adjacent to the village to check up on Samir's brother, and that the physician warned about obstruction of the arteries due to the large amount of meat he used to eat at home from which he would hear the scum of the sheep.

After the father of the beautiful Lamya had repeatedly refused Samir's asking for her hand in marriage, the father at last agreed, after being urged by his wife and children. They surely were taking account of the father's strong authority over the members of the family, but they were keen to protect the honor of the girl. Abd al-Fattah, Lamya's eldest brother, said to his mother: "To protect the honor of the girl is to get her married."

The mother said: "Yes, my son. How many times shall I hear this talk from you? Go to your father and try to convince him."

Abd al-Fattah's father was convinced, but he had hoped that the son of a wealthy man would ask for Lamya's hand in marriage, so that he might be able to improve his economic situation.

With gladness dancing on their faces, Samir's parents, his four brothers and four sisters headed for the home of Abd al-Fattah's father to discuss when to draw up the marriage contract. Samir was excited.

When they banged the faded, rusty knocker, Abd al-Fattah's father opened the door, saying with a fixed, earnest gaze: "Welcome, your coming is an honor for us."

Samir's father and the members of his family sat down on old sofas in a medium-size room next to the small kitchen.

Samir, with a movement of his head which may not have been intended, saw her—this was the first time he had seen her for many months—and his heart began to beat faster, while she was fixing the coffee with cardamom in the kitchen. With a greeting and welcoming smiles, Lamya and her brothers turned toward Samir's father and his family.

Samir's excitement increased; the sweat began pouring down his forehead, as he took longing but discreet glances at Lamya; he was indulging in the hope that in the not-too-distant future she would be his wife and the mother of his children.

But no sooner had she approached him, carrying the tray of coffee in order to honor him and his family with it, than he collapsed on the floor.

With astonishment and in a strong, earnest tone, Samir's father said: "What is the matter with you, Samir? The coffee that Miss Lamya has made for you in honor of writing the marriage contract is waiting for you."

Samir did not get up. He lay motionless. They took his pulse, and discovered that his life had left him.

A Short Statement of the Author's Biography and Thought

Biography: Taysir Nashif is a professor, researcher, author, translator and reviser. He was born in Tayiba located between Haifa, Jaffa and Nabulus in the Holy Land. He earned a B.A. degree in Arabic language and literature and political science, an M.A. degree in international relations from the University of Jerusalem and an M.A. degree in May 1969 in Islamic studies from the University of Toronto in Canada. In 1974, he obtained a Ph.D. degree in political science from the State University of New York at Binghamton.

In 1976, he was appointed as assistant professor at the Department of Sociology in Oran, Algeria. From 1980-81, he was appointed as political affairs officer in Office of General Assembly Affairs of the United Nations in New York. In 1982, he served as deputy-chief of the UN Arabic Verbatim Reporting Section. Besides his administrative functions, he served as translator, editor and reviser of the records of the meetings held by the UN Security Council, the General Assembly and other UN forums. In 1996 he became chief of the Section. He retired in 2002.

Dr. Nashif is or was a member in the following scholarly forums:

- Middle East Studies Association (MESA).
- American Political Science Association (APSA).
- Association of Third World Studies (ATWS).
- American Association of University Professors (AAUP).
- Third World Foundation (TWF).
- American Association of Teachers of Arabic (AATA).
- Arab-American University Graduates (AAUG).
- American Translators Association (ATA).
- American Historical Association (AHA).

He attended annual conferences held by these and other forums in which he made presentations in his fields of specialization. Some of these presentations were included in the published proceedings of such conferences.

Taysir Nashif is a prolific writer. He is the author of a number of books and articles and studies published in both Arabic and English in the United States, Europe, the Arab world, Australia and other areas. These writings mainly deal with conventional and nuclear armament and disarmament, political, social and cultural change in the developing world, rise, decline and fall of civilizations, including factors of social, cultural, economic, scientific and technological underdevelopment.

Books published in Arabic:

- *Al-'Asliha an-Nawawiyya fii ('Israa'iil (Nuclear Weapons in Israel)* (Beirut: 'Al-Mu'assasa al-'Arabiyya li-al-Diraasaat wa-al-Nashr, 1990).
- *Al-'Arab wa-al-'Aalam fii al-Qarn al-Qaadim (The Arabs and the World in the Coming Century)* (Nazareth: At-Talaa'i', 1998).
- *Mufakkiruun Filastiiniyuun fii al-Qarn al-'Ishriin (Palestinian Thinkers in the Twentieth Century)* (Nazareth: 'At-Talaa'i', 1999).
- *As-Sulta wa-al-Hurriyya al-Fikriyya wa-al-Mujtama'* (Authority, Intellectual Freedom and Society) (Beirut: Al-Mu'assasa al-'Arabiyya li-al-Diraasaat wa-al-Nashr, 2001).
- *Az-Za'aamataan as-Siyasiyytaan al-'Arabiyya wa-al-Yahudiyya fii Filastiin: Dirasa Muwaarina (The Arab and Jewish Political Leaderhip in Palestine: A Comparative Study)* (Beirut: Al-Mu'assasa al-'Arabiyya li-al-Diraasaat wa-al-Nashr, 2002).
- *As-Sulta wa-al-Fikr wa-al-Taghayyur al-'Igtimaa'ii (Authority, Thought and Social Change)* ('Ammaan: 'Azmina, 2003).
- *An-Nashaat al-Fikrii wa-al-Taghayyur al-'Igtimaa'ii* ('Ammaan: 'Azmina, 2005).
- *Mukhtaaraat min ash-Shi'r al-'Arabii al-Mu'aasir (Selections from Contemporary Arab Poetry)*, edited by Taysir Nashif and Kaiser 'Afiif (Princeton: Publications of Al-Haraka ash-Shi'riyya, 2006).
- *Tilal wa-Dhilaal* (Hills and Shadows) (Patterson, NJ: Olive Publishing, 2007).

Books published in English:

- *The Palestine Arab and Jewish Political Leaderships: A Comparative Study* (New York: Asia, 1979).

- *Nuclear Warfare in the Middle East: Dimensions and Responsibilities* (Princeton: Kingston Press, 1984).
- *Nuclear Weapons in Israel* (New Delhi: APH, 1996).
- *Government, the Intellectual and Society in the Third World* (Kolkata: Academic Publishers, 2004).
- *Society, Intellectuals and Cultural Change in the Developing Countries* (New York: iUniverse, 2006).
- *Weakness of Nuclear Deterrence in the Near East: Israel and Nuclear Weapons* (Berlin: LAMBERT Academic Publishing, 2010).
- *Social Justice and Intellectual Suppression* (Bloomington, IN: Authorhouse, 2011).

Of the publications in which articles and researches have been published are the following: *Al-Mawaakib (Processions), Menalmuheetlelkaleej (From the Ocean to the Gulf), 'Aklaam (Pens), Doroob (Roads), Safsaf, Majallat al-Haraka ash-Shi'riyya (The Journal of the Movement of Poetry), Al-Hewar (Dialogue), Jusuur (Bridges), Shu'uun Filastiniyya (Palestinian Affairs), Al-Hiwaar (Dialogue), Al-'Ufuq al-'Arabii (The Arab Horizon),'Ufuq (Horizon), Al-Muhaajir (The Emigrant), Difaaf (Banks), 'Alwaah (Boards), 'Al-Mustaqbal (Future), 'Ammaan ('Ammaan), 'Al-Majalla al-Thaqaafiyya (The Cultural Journal), Rose al-Yusuf, Sawt Dahesh, Dahesh Voice, 'Al-Quds al-'Arabii (Arab Jerusalem), 'Al-Bayaan (Statement), 'Al-Jadiid (The New), Mawaaqif (Positions), 'Al-Hakiim (The Physician), Sawt al-'Uruuba (The Arab Voice), 'Al-Minassa al-'Arabiyya (The Arab Platform), 'Awtaar (Strings), 'Al-Muntaqid (The Critic), 'Adabiyyaat (Literature), 'Al-Mirbad, 'Al-'Arabii al-Hurr (The Free Arab), 'Aqlaam (Pens), Diiwaan al-'Arab (The Arabs' Divan), 'Al-'ajniha (The Wings), Samaa' (A Sky), Tranzinu, 'Al-Fawaaniis (Lanterns), Shi'r wa-'Adab (Poetry and Literature), Masaaraat (Paths), Sakhirin (Mockers), Latef, AkherKhabarUSA (Recent NewsUSA), Nashiij al-Mahaabir al-'Adabiyya (The Literary Nashiij Inkwells), Triond, ArabNews (Canada), Afnanonline, Loblab (English Ivy), Ebdaaa (Creation), Madarate (Orbits), Tfaneen(Versatility), Omraalklam (Princes of Speech), Naseej (A Woven Fabric), 'Uud an-Nadd (An-Nadd Twig), AIRS, Cirta, Orook, Al-Manahel (The Springs), Bashaa'ir (Good Tidings),Latef, Arab-ewriters, Ansaq (Modes), Inana, Al-'Arab Weekly Newspaper, Baaab (Door), Al-Watan Voice (The Voice of the Homeland), Post Poems, Sadaa al-Mahjar (The Echo of the Place of Emigration),Al-Sdaqa (Friendship), ArabsWATA, At-Talii'a (Vanguard), 'Ashri'a (Sails), Al-Nuuraanii (The Luminous), Deyar alnagab (The Naqab Homeland), Qadaayaanaa (Our Issues), 'Ashtar, Grenc (The*

Green Basis), Besan, Absso, Safahaat (Sheets), Al-Mar'a (Woman), Freearabi, Al-Majalla al-Thaqaafiyya (The Cultural Journal), Al-Jisr (The Bridge), Alraafidmag, Hdrmut, Albawaba (The Portal), Hewar.Khayma (Dialogue-A Tent), Maakom (With you), Almothaqaf (The educated), Marabicfriends (The Academy for the Friends of the Arabic Language), Alodaba (Men of Letters), JMA3 (Society of the Cultural Association), Arabs48, Al-Qaf, Matarmatar (Rainrain), Kikah, ISF, Journal of Third World Studies.

Thought: In the following is a brief statement of the author's thought.

Any social phenomenon in the more general sense, namely, of cultural, political, economic, psychological and historical dimensions, has relationship to other social phenomena. However, relations between such phenomena differ in terms of weakness or strength following factors, including their vertical (historical) location and their horizontal (present) location. Past is one component of the present and the future, and present is a component of the future.

Social structures at the country level as well as the regional and international levels are in a continuing interaction. In this structural interaction, the more influential factors determine the direction of change.

All peoples pass through stages of growth. Developing peoples in the countries of Asia, Africa and Latin America, however, undergo a greater suffering from scientific, social, political, economic and industrial backwardness because of internal and external factors among which relations of reciprocal relations exist.

Woman in all parts of the world are wronged and subjugated; ill-treatment of the Arab and Muslim women is remarkable. In order to achieve the desired social progress in the wide sense, lifting ill-treatment of women must be one of the items of agenda on strategy of action for social and psychological change leading to social and scientific progress. No real progress can be achieved with the emancipation of women.

Developing peoples living in these continents can catch up with, and suppress, the progress of the peoples of the developed countries. To achieve that aim, the developing countries should regain their self-confidence, as loss of self-confidence is one of the most important factors in the underdevelopment of the developing peoples.

Western social thought is flawed by some defects, one of the more important of which is to attempt to explain social phenomena in the wider sense with only one factor. Marxism and Freudism, for example, have tried to explain phenomenon with one factor or one major factor. This is one of the important reasons for the defect that flaws Western understanding of the dynamics of human life.

All of the activities of human societies are restricted or paralyzed by socio-political constraints. Arab societies, as all human societies, suffer from such constraints. Constraint basically means lack of meeting or accommodation of the intellectual, emotional and material needs and wishes. Socio-political constraints have reciprocal relationship to the intellectual, economic and financial situation, to value systems and to concepts, visions, imagination and expectations. Mechanisms should be developed to remove constraints or, at least, to alleviate them. One of the more important mechanisms which many of the developing countries are lacking is a mechanism to exercise democracy, to exercise a serious dialogue, and to remove the barriers which hinder intellectual communication.

As a large amount of thought deals with the existing congestions, in various fields, from which human groups are suffering, concern with issues which the people's interests require giving consideration to them diminishes, a matter which comes at the expense of the people's interests.

As to democracy, it is predicated on participation, intellectual pluralism and making alternatives and options available. Spread of democracy would encourage intellectual emancipation and creativity.

A factor which prevents or delays progress in its various aspects or dimensions in the developing world is the patriarchal system. Tribal, familial and sectarian systems have weakened the development of democratic states.

A permanent characteristic of human relations and conditions in the various fields of human existence is that such relations and conditions are in constant dynamic change. Depending on the intensity of the dynamic interaction among the social, psychological, and natural factors, such change may be slow or quick, and little or considerable.

Given this, it is extremely difficult, if not impossible, to achieve the desired change without giving, at the same time, consideration to all of the factors in the constantly changing human relations and conditions.